WHERE'S DOM?

Join Dom Cummings and his pals on a sightseeing tour of Britain!

IZZY MISSING

WELBECK

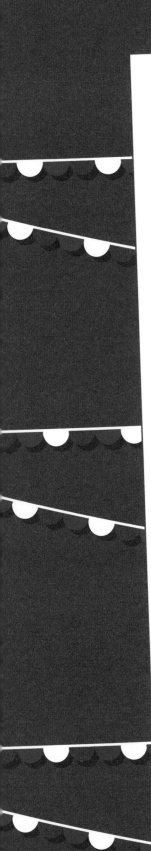

Hello minions dear friends,

My name is Dominic Cummings. You may have heard of me before as one of the many people serving you, the great British public, to Make Britain Great Again. (I just came up with that... it's got a nice ring to it, doesn't it? Must make a note to pass it on to BJ at our next pub sesh.)

Over the many months of lockdown, just like the rest of you, I've hardly even set foot outside of my small, cramped Islington mansion. However, it seems like wherever I go, whatever I do, the dangerous Mainstream Media™ and the liberal elites who run it think I'm up to something dastardly and nefarious.

Nothing could be further from the truth! Look into my eyes. Deeper... Deeper... Is this the sort of face that could ever lie to you?

Exactly. So, my fellow good citizens, here is an honest and truthful account of my time over the past few months. Think of me as the Forrest Gump of lockdown – always popping up where you least expect me. Have I been in the wrong place at the wrong time occasionally? Perhaps. But also definitely 100% not. And I can assure you, my actions are what anyone else would have done in my very, very, *very* special situation.

Cheerio chaps, your servant and friend,

Dom

ITALIAN SKI SLOPES

LIVERPOOL V ATLETICO MADRID

CHELTENHAM FESTIVAL

THE M1 SERVICES TO DURHAM

BARNARD CASTLE

THE SUPERMARKET QUEUE

VE DAY VILLAGE FÊTE

OUTSIDE DOM'S HOUSE

THE DOWNING STREET ROSE GARDEN

DOWN THE PARK

DURDLE DOOR

A CHEEKY PUB LOCK-IN

EXTRA HIDDEN OBJECTS

ITALIAN SKI SLOPES

- [ ] A picnic
- [ ] Someone blowing their nose
- [ ] A snowman
- [ ] A skier with only one ski
- [ ] A partier passed out in the snow with a drink in both hands
- [ ] Someone wearing double earmuffs to block out the karaoke
- [ ] Someone eating a big plate of sausages
- [ ] A skier in an EU ski suit

LIVERPOOL V ATLETICO MADRID

- [ ] A paramedic in a hazmat suit
- [ ] A beachball
- [ ] An unfortunate Everton fan
- [ ] Someone eating a delicious pie with bovril
- [ ] Someone getting a red card
- [ ] A VAR TV screen getting some treatment from the fans
- [ ] A Dominic Cummings cardboard cut out – one of many that have been seen around the world
- [ ] The Premier League trophy

CHELTENHAM FESTIVAL

- [ ] A single hand sanitiser unit – why would you need more?
- [ ] An elaborate feathered hat
- [ ] Someone drunk and passed out on the floor
- [ ] A streaker
- [ ] Where's Wally? fancy dress
- [ ] A jockey ready to go on the classic British pastime of fox-hunting
- [ ] Someone tearing up a losing bet
- [ ] A horse drinking a pint – why not, everyone else is doing it!

THE M1 SERVICES TO DURHAM

- [ ] A McDonald's bag
- [ ] A fruit machine being stolen
- [ ] An over-excited dog chasing its owner
- [ ] A child throwing a water balloon
- [ ] A motorbike side-car
- [ ] An NHS rainbow sign in a car window
- [ ] A business meeting
- [ ] Someone pouring whiskey into their coffee

BARNARD CASTLE

- [ ] A pair of misplaced glasses
- [ ] The Barnard Castle sign
- [ ] A pair of binoculars
- [ ] A woman locked in the stocks
- [ ] A lifejacket
- [ ] An eye test exam for Dom to take
- [ ] A man dressed as a king
- [ ] A horse running loose

So, you think you can find us too?! Pah!!

THE SUPERMARKET QUEUE

- [ ] Someone well protected in a gasmask
- [ ] Someone stealing oranges
- [ ] Someone even more well protected in a suit of armour
- [ ] Someone drinking a squirt of alcoholic hand sanitiser
- [ ] Someone demonstrating Boris's cake-ism by holding a cake and eating a slice too
- [ ] An adult in a trolley seat
- [ ] Someone wrapped up like a toilet paper Mummy
- [ ] An Easter egg

VE DAY VILLAGE FÊTE

- ❑ A barbecue on fire
- ❑ A dog running off with a string of sausages
- ❑ A TV showing the Queen's address
- ❑ A Winston Churchill lookalike
- ❑ A well-decorated soldier with almost too many medals
- ❑ Someone at the wrong party wearing lederhosen!
- ❑ A Brazilian carnival dancer
- ❑ A delicious Union Jack cake

OUTSIDE DOM'S HOUSE

- ❑ A policeman issuing a lockdown fine
- ❑ Dom's misplaced glasses
- ❑ A photographer with an old-school Kodak
- ❑ A Black Lives Matter protester
- ❑ A VE Day reveler still going strong many days later
- ❑ Bad Vlad Putin
- ❑ A hard-looking bouncer
- ❑ An Amazon package

THE DOWNING STREET ROSE GARDEN

- ❑ The Forbidden Fruit
- ❑ Larry the Downing Street cat looking very relaxed
- ❑ A clever fox getting into the garden party food
- ❑ The Chancellor's red box
- ❑ Someone having their temperature checked
- ❑ A rat!
- ❑ David Cameron
- ❑ Garden shears

DOWN THE PARK

- ❑ A bottle of suntan lotion
- ❑ Someone drinking Pimms
- ❑ A hand-sanitiser station
- ❑ A safety-conscious adult skateboarding with a helmet on
- ❑ Someone playing an accordion
- ❑ A kite
- ❑ A frisbee
- ❑ A policeman trying and failing to enforce social distancing

DURDLE DOOR

- ❑ An overflowing rubbish bin
- ❑ A social-distancing 2 metre warning sign
- ❑ Someone reading Machiavelli's *The Prince*
- ❑ A fisherman straining to catch a massive fish
- ❑ Someone completely buried in the sand, except their head
- ❑ Someone with just their head buried in the sand (unlike any world leaders…)
- ❑ An adult wearing armbands
- ❑ The only person wearing a facemask

A CHEEKY PUB LOCK-IN

- ❑ A Leave Means Leave poster
- ❑ Someone doing tequila suicide (squeezing lime in the eye before drinking their tequila)
- ❑ A dog drinking beer out of a dog bowl
- ❑ Someone pouring their own pint
- ❑ A truly original "We've Missed You" message on a chalkboard
- ❑ A bottle of champagne
- ❑ Someone drawing on someone else's face
- ❑ Sajid Javid

You can't find us four proper lads!!

In March, Dom took off on a lads' trip to the Dolomites for a cheeky getaway. Good times were had by all - they even managed to get in a couple hours of skiing before popping in to the bar for drinks.

Dom just managed to get back from Europe before flights were cancelled. He was sure that it was Liverpool's year to win the Champions League, so he organised a trip to Anfield with his mates to see them beat Atletico Madrid. What could go wrong?

Dom thought a trip to Cheltenham was just the ticket to take his mind off this strange new virus. Apparently there had been COBRA meetings held about it, but Boris wasn't bothered. He said it would all be fine if we just washed our hands a bit more.

Feeling a little iffy, Dom decided it was time to get out of London and leg it across the country. Fortunately, he never once stopped the entire way to Durham...

Dom and his chums have decided to go on a test-drive to Barnard Castle, which has coincided with a medieval re-enactment. He only got out for a minute to stretch his legs, though - honestly!

Back to full health at last, Dom was feeling peckish. Plus, he had to stock up for the big VE Day street party he was meant to be hosting!

SPAG ROLLS

It was VE Day - a welcome distraction - and the whole country was out to celebrate. Dom had his dancing shoes on and was wondering if he could get anyone to join his conga line this year.

Dom couldn't believe it! The liberal elites were after him - again! - just because he'd travelled from his Islington townhouse to one of the many cottages on his family farm during the lockdown he himself had designed. At least he knew the country understood and were 100% on his side.

It was Dom's big day! He was super excited to finally have the eyes of the nation on him, for once. Benedict Cumberbatch - eat your heart out! But even though he was sure everyone was going to love him, he was still a bit nervous and is hiding from the cameras.

Suns out, guns out - that's another one of Dom's great slogans! And with a heatwave hitting Britain, Dom and his mates wasted no time getting down to the park to soak in some rays, crack open a couple of tinnies and show off their sexy dad bods.

With summer on its way, Dom decided a jaunt to Durdle Door was just the thing to lift his spirits. He was sure it would be easy to social distance on the lovely, big beach.

The lockdown was nearly over - at last! To celebrate, Dom and his pals managed to convince their local to have a cheeky sneaky lock-in. They promised it would be a very quiet and private party. Everyone was going to social distance, and the pub would hardly even know they had been there.

SOLUTIONS

○ People   ○ Extra hidden objects

ITALIAN SKI SLOPES

LIVERPOOL V ATLETICO MADRID

CHELTENHAM FESTIVAL

THE M1 SERVICES TO DURHAM

BARNARD CASTLE

THE SUPERMARKET QUEUE

VE DAY VILLAGE FÊTE

OUTSIDE DOM'S HOUSE

THE DOWNING STREET ROSE GARDEN

DOWN THE PARK

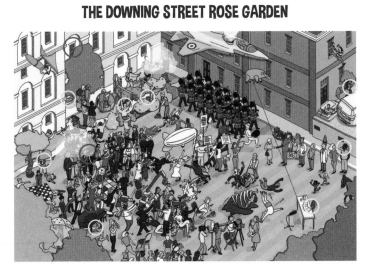

DURDLE DOOR

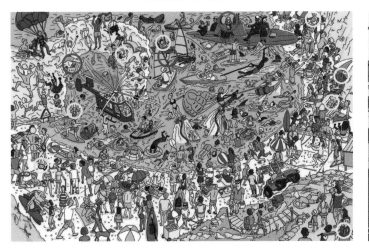

A CHEEKY PUB LOCK-IN

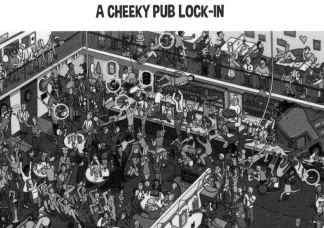

Illustrations by Wings Illustration
www.wingsillustration.com

Published in 2020 by Welbeck
an imprint of Welbeck Non-Fiction Limited,
part of Welbeck Publishing Group
20 Mortimer Street London W1T 3JW

A CIP catalogue record for this book is available from the British Library

ISBN 978-1-78739-582-4

Printed in Spain

1 3 5 7 9 10 8 6 4 2